Dedicated to the Print Room, where the miracle begins.

Special thanks to Alexis Deacon, Arthur Vergani, Becky Palmer, Chris Duriez, Elys Dolan, Jess Lau, John Wiliams, Katherina Manolessou, Linda Lai, Martin Salibury, May Fung, Pam Smy, Phemie Chong, Shelley Jackson, Ziggy Hanaor, Aco, Floating Projects, JCCAC and the Six Bells Massive.

Nomads

Text © Ziggy Hanaor and Kinchoi Lam
Illustration © Kinchoi Lam

British Library Cataloguing-in-Publication Data.

A CIP record for this book is available from the British Library
ISBN: 978-1-80066-032-8

First published in 2022 in the UK, 2023 in the USA.

Cicada Books Ltd
48 Burghley Road
London, NW5 1UE
www.cicadabooks.co.uk

All rights reserved. No part of this publication may be reproduced stored in a retrieval system or transmitted in any form or by any means; electronic, mechanical, photocopying, recording or otherwise, without prior permission of the publisher.

Printed in Poland on FSC certified paper.

Nomads
Life on the move

Kinchoi Lam

Contents

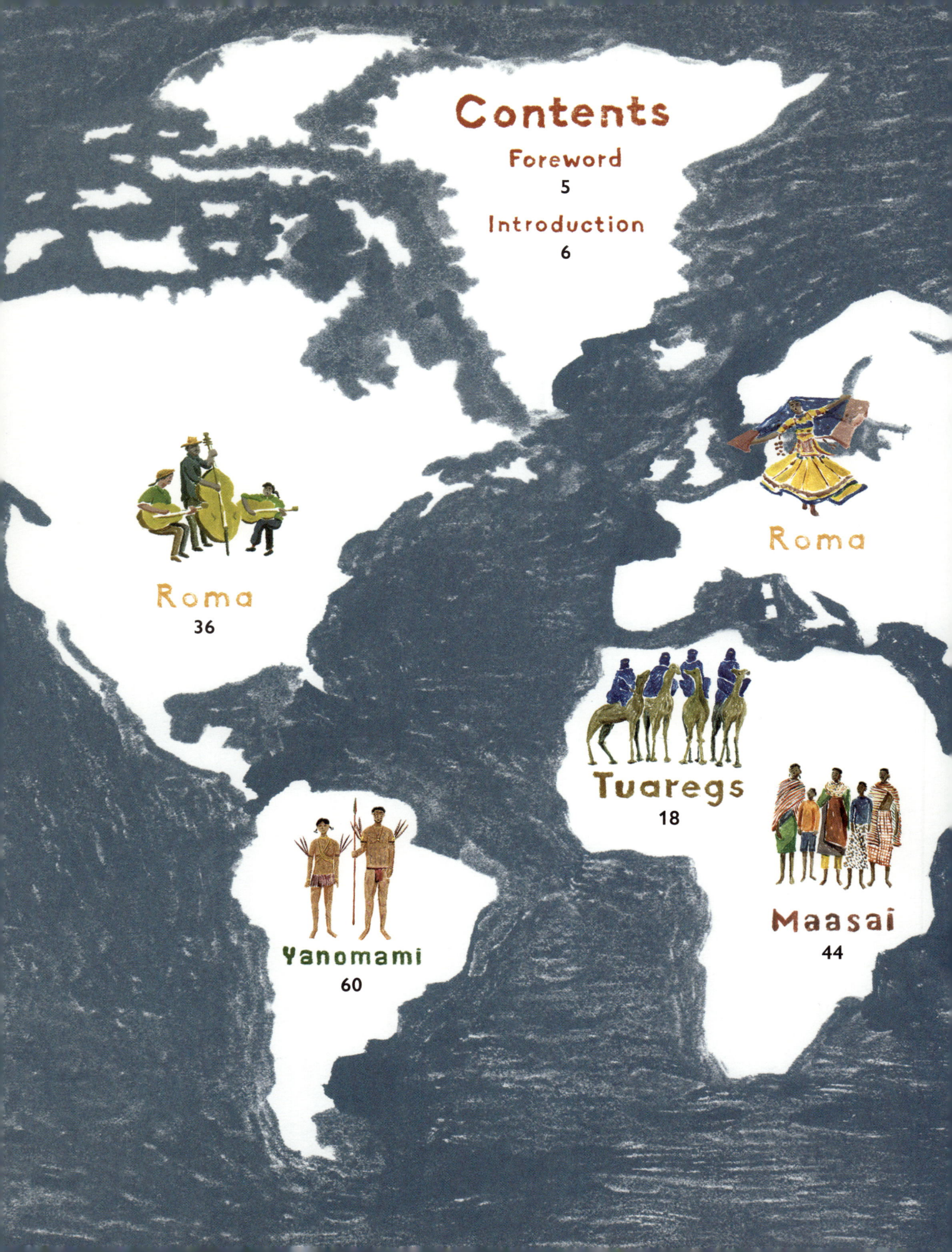

Foreword
5

Introduction
6

Roma
36

Roma

Tuaregs
18

Maasai
44

Yanomami
60

Nenets
28

Mongolian Nomads
8

Sama-Bajau
52

Conclusion
68
Glossary
72

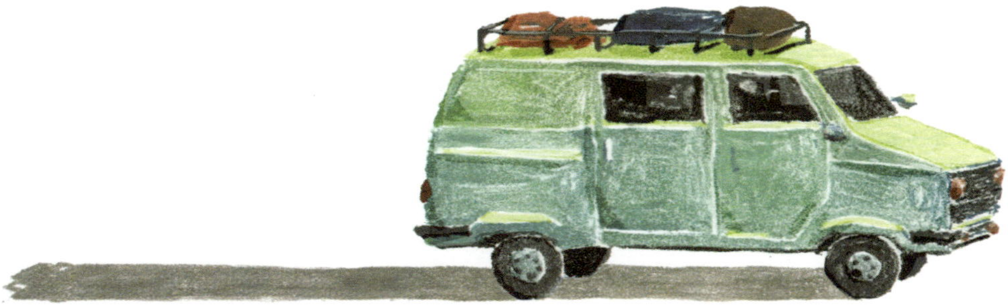

Foreword

I was inspired to write this book during a journey to the heart of the Sahara Desert. It seemed no matter how deep into the desert we drove, there were groups of people herding animals and carrying water to temporary accommodation that was far off the electrical grid. I am a seasoned traveller – I have moved country and house more times than I can count, but I've always had four walls and a roof that I could call my own. The more I thought about it, the more it made me question; what makes a home, and how have our lives become so reliant on objects and walls, and so separated from the realities of weather and nature?

Nomadic cultures rely on knowledge that has been passed down through the generations to keep them safe in the wide world. They know how to navigate the winds of the Arctic tundra to find grass for their reindeer, or how to differentiate between thousands of plants in the Amazon rainforest, recognising which will nourish and which will heal. They are great architects, building and dismantling a home in a single day, and often skilled crafts-people; adept at blacksmithing or weaving. Community and religion often play a big role in their lives, providing structures made not of solid walls but of tradition, respect and spirituality.

This book explores different ways of living, which are more relevant now than ever. As we rethink our lifestyles in the face of global warming, it is important to look to cultures that are more in tune with the environment; that fit within an ecosystem, instead of controlling it.

I'd like to think that in a world where walls, boundaries and possessions mean a lot less, it is easier to have an open mind about how we can protect our real home; this incredible planet.

-- Kinchoi Lam

Life on the Move: An Introduction

Once upon a time (up until 12,000 years ago), all humans were nomadic. We roamed the earth, hunting for food, and occasionally being hunted ourselves. We moved in small tribes, telling each other stories of spirits and ancestors, and gradually creating individual cultures — ways of living, ways of eating, ways of expressing ourselves and ways of coexisting with our environments.

Gradually, humans began to settle down, building permanent houses, growing crops and domesticating animals such as goats, pigs, cows and chickens. This was called the Neolithic Revolution. Settled life offered the promise of security and wealth, and most humans gave up their nomadic ways. Children were helpful in tending to the fields, and soon there was a population explosion. Governments and nations emerged, bringing order and structure to the expanding communities.

Despite the temptations of settled life, some nomadic societies continued to thrive. Often, their flexible lifestyles gave them military advantages. The Scythians, who lived around 5 BCE, were fearsome horse-riding warriors. In the 12th century, the Mongols ruled the largest empire in history, with lands that stretched from modern day Ukraine to Southern China.

However, the past 100 years have made nomadic lifestyles ever more difficult. Crop farming means that a lot of land is privately owned, and people are not allowed to roam freely across it. Mining and industrialisation have degraded the quality of natural environments, making it harder to hunt and to herd. Governments often force nomads to settle down so that they may be more easily monitored and controlled.

Even so, against all odds, certain nomadic communities around the world have managed to hold onto their traditional ways of life. These nomadic cultures can be divided into three categories: Hunter gatherers, like the Sama Bajau, usually move through a relatively small area which they know very well; searching for the animals and plants that provide their food and livelihood. Pastoral nomads, like the Nenets or Mongolian nomads, herd grazing livestock – cattle or reindeer. They migrate in large circles, following vegetation growth as the seasons change. Tinker/trader nomads, like the Roma, work alongside settled society, selling goods or working as labourers, but keeping a mobile way of life.

This book looks at the lifestyles and traditions of seven nomadic societies that are still active today. They were chosen for the variety of their cultures and the environments that they inhabit, but they have a lot in common. All nomadic peoples have a portable lifestyle. This means a tent/yurt, or other living structure that can easily be put up and dismantled. They have minimal possessions – every item they carry with them must serve a purpose, or it becomes dead weight. They often thrive in extreme landscapes, where there is still plenty of open land that has not yet been privatised, and they have unique knowledge of their home's ecosystem and biodiversity, managing it and protecting it, so that it may continue to provide for them.

Nomadic cultures can teach us a lot about how to live more sustainably. Their traditions, which are often not written down, stretch back thousands of years, deep into the heart of human history. They offer us a glimpse into who we were before we became who we are. There is much inspiration to be found in life on the move.

Mongolian Nomads

Mongolia is a very sparsely populated country; three million people live in a country four times the size of Germany. Mongolia is high, cold and windy with extreme temperatures ranging from -30°C in the winter to 48°C in the summer. Vast grasslands called steppes stretch across an otherwise empty landscape.

Throughout history, Mongolia has been ruled by nomadic emperors, the most famous being Genghis Khan, who governed the largest land empire in history from 1206 to 1227. Up until 1960, three quarters of the population of Mongolia was nomadic. Today, that figure has shrunk to one third. Their lifestyle, which revolves around the grazing patterns of their livestock, has remained unchanged for centuries.

Ger Life

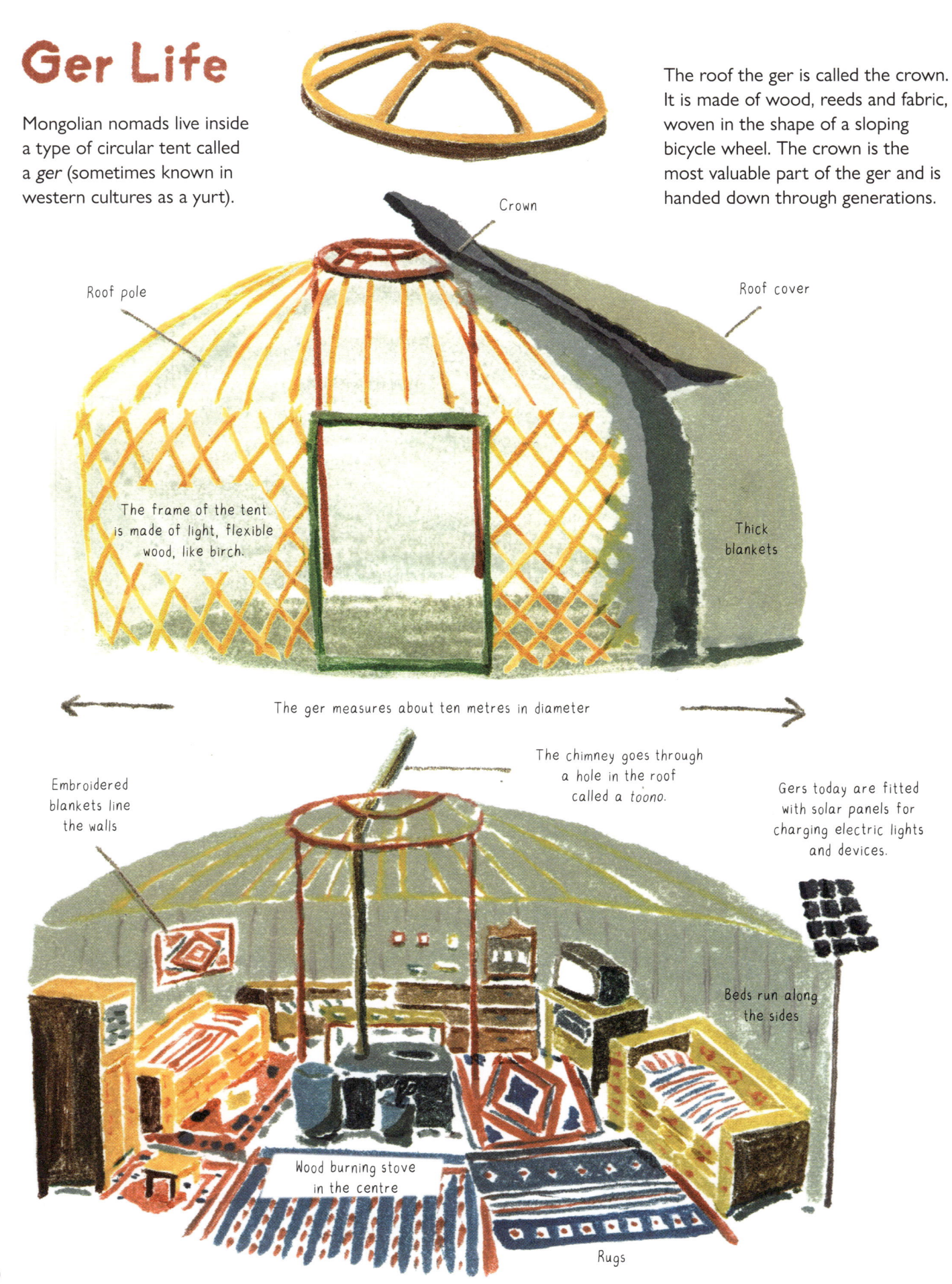

Mongolian nomads live inside a type of circular tent called a *ger* (sometimes known in western cultures as a yurt).

The roof the ger is called the crown. It is made of wood, reeds and fabric, woven in the shape of a sloping bicycle wheel. The crown is the most valuable part of the ger and is handed down through generations.

Crown

Roof pole

Roof cover

The frame of the tent is made of light, flexible wood, like birch.

Thick blankets

← The ger measures about ten metres in diameter →

Embroidered blankets line the walls

The chimney goes through a hole in the roof called a *toono*.

Gers today are fitted with solar panels for charging electric lights and devices.

Beds run along the sides

Wood burning stove in the centre

Rugs

Powerful winds blow constantly across the steppe. The flexible framework of the ger has been designed to withstand the gales and the temperature extremes.

The walls are made of thick, felted sheep's wool for insulation. Their circular shape makes them able to resist winds from any direction, and the *toono* roof opening allows fresh air to enter.

In the rainy season, a moat is dug around the ger so that it doesn't become unstable.

Most gers can be assembled within three hours and dismantled in one. They are then carried to the next destination on the back of a yak or a camel.

Moving days are very important. The head of the family will wear his nicest clothes. Any quarrel whilst preparing for the move is considered a bad omen.

Living

The nomads travel in groups with anywhere between 100 and 1,000 animals – mostly sheep and goats, but also yaks, dogs, horses and camels. A nomad's wealth is measured by how many horses and livestock they own.

In the north of the country, the nomads will only move a few times a year to allow their herds to graze. They move down to the lowland pastures in the autumn and up to the mountains in the spring.

There are hundreds of lakes. The biggest one is Lake Uvs.

Ulaanbaatar (the capital)

The centre of the country is mountainous and forested.

The Gobi Desert in the south covers 30% of the country.

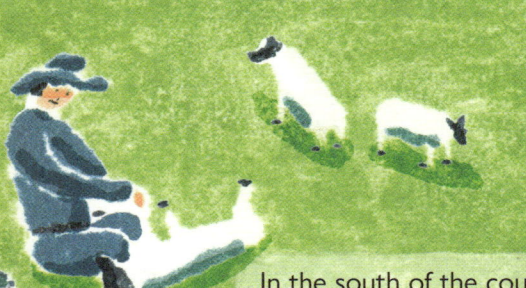

In the south of the country, where water is scarce, herders will move at least 20 times a year.

Although they are not permanent, the gers are comfortably furnished with sofas, furniture and even a fridge and a television. Some other traditional homewares include:

Containers for food and drink

Wood-burning stoves for cooking and heating

Small cabinet with a bowl used as a sink

Meaningful family photos

A small Buddhist shrine

Futons to sleep on

Stools

Sheep anklebones called 'shagai', which are used like dice in a game

The Mongol horse is a small, powerful native breed.

Sometime a saddle is used, and sometimes the horse is ridden bareback.

Their hooves are almost never shod.

Traditionally, Mongolian nomads herded and protected their cattle on horseback. Although herding these days is often done on motorbike, the nomads still take great pride in their horse-riding skills, and most families keep a few horses.

Clothing

Mongolian nomads wear a heavy, tunic-like coat called a *del*, which is fastened with a long, colourful belt.

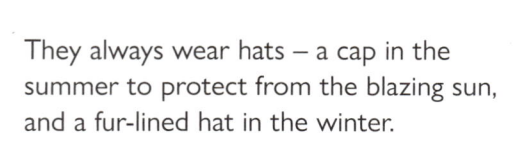

They always wear hats – a cap in the summer to protect from the blazing sun, and a fur-lined hat in the winter.

Traditional boots are made of leather with a toe that curls upwards. In the winter, they are lined with thick felt.

Food

The nomads rely on their animals for food. The summer months are known as 'white months'. The female livestock produce a lot of milk, and the diet is mostly dairy based – milk, yogurt and cheeses. The winter months are known as 'red months', as the diet is mostly meat-based.

Buuz is a dumpling filled with steamed meat.

Khorkhog is a casserole cooked with hot stones.

Airag is a drink made of fermented mare's milk.

In western Mongolia, Kazakh nomads practice the art of eagle hunting. In winter months, when food is in short supply, they will ride on horseback, carrying great golden eagles on their arms. The eagles will fly off and bring back their prey of foxes and hares.

Future

Climate change has had a big impact on the weather in Mongolia. A *dzud* is a weather pattern in which a hot, dry summer is followed by a harsh winter. This weather pattern is becoming more common, and it is disastrous for the livestock that the nomads rely on, as the animals cannot fatten up in the summer, and are then unable to withstand the bitter winter.

In 2009, over 10,000 cattle died in a dzud, forcing many nomads to abandon their traditional ways of life and move to the Mongolian capital, Ulaanbaatar.

On the outskirts of the city, a huge ger-city expands each year. These 'ger-slums' are not connected to proper sewage or electric systems, and must burn coal for heating and cooking, creating a big air-pollution problem.

Even the herders who choose stay on the steppe often encourage their children to pursue education and a settled way of life, so that they may have a more secure future.

Tuaregs

The Tuareg people inhabit one of the harshest environments on the planet, the Sahara Desert. For centuries, they have travelled in camel caravans across an area that stretches over two million square kilometres across lands belonging to Libya, Mali, Burkina Faso and Niger.

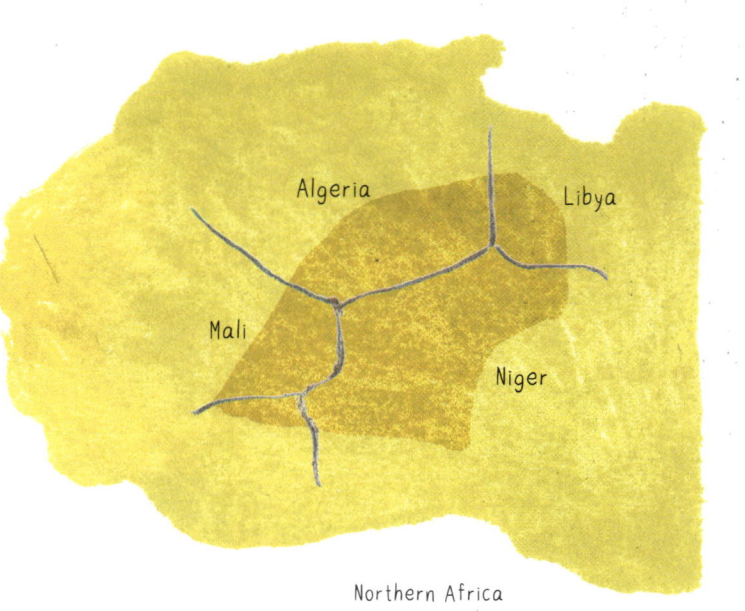

Northern Africa

A camel caravan is a train of camels carrying passengers and goods along a defined route.

For many hundreds of years, The Tuareg had complete control over North African trade routes. They would bring salt, gold, ivory and, for a period, slaves, across the desert to the ports, so they could be sold and transported around the world.

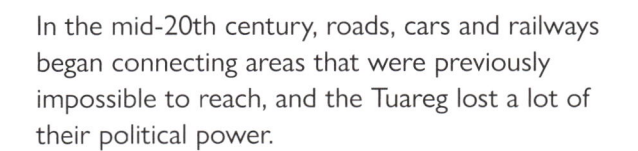

In the mid-20th century, roads, cars and railways began connecting areas that were previously impossible to reach, and the Tuareg lost a lot of their political power.

Tuareg is an Arabic term, whose origins are unknown. The Tuaregs call themselves *Imohag*, which translates as 'free men'. They are also sometimes known as the 'blue people', as the men wear a distinctive indigo headscarf called a *tagelmust*, which dyes their skin blue.

"A house is a coffin for the living."
-- Tuareg proverb

Living

Whilst travelling, the Tuareg live in tents that can easily be packed away and carried to the next destination. Tuareg tents are made of arched wooden frames covered with goatskins. Inside the tent, woven straw mats line the walls to keep the space cool and to prevent sand from getting inside. The mats are also used as dividers, separating out private spaces.

They travel in clans made up of a number of families, led by a chief called the *amghar*. Wealthier nobles tend to live in bigger, more impressive tents.

The phrase 'making a tent' means to get married in the Tuareg language.

Unlike many traditional societies, women are treated as equals in Tuareg culture. When a couple gets married, a tent is built for them, which is named after the wife. She owns the tent, and if the couple later gets divorced (which is commonplace and not frowned upon), the man must leave the tent.

A *takabart* is a temporary hut for the winter.

A *taghazamt* is a house made of adobe mud for a longer stay.

Food

The Tuareg diet mostly consists of dairy, fruit and grains like couscous. Meat is only eaten on special occasions.

Cheeses and yogurts are made from goat's milk, including *eghajira*, which is a drink made of millet, goats cheese, dates and milk. Camel milk is also popular.

Taguella is a flatbread that is cooked on charcoal and then buried under the hot sand.

Atai is a green tea that is drunk throughout the day with plenty of sugar.

Desert life means that water must be carried at all times. Bottles used to be made of goatskin, but now it is more common to see people carrying water in the inner tube of a truck tyre.

Religion and traditions

Although Tuareg people now practice Islam, they also hold onto their traditional, pre-Islamic beliefs. They tell stories about ancestors and spirits, many of whom are female. Evil ghosts called *djinns* must be protected against. Fortunes are told using cowrie shells, mirrors and lizards.

Society

Tuareg society is very hierarchical. Wealthy nobles/warriors run the camel caravans and are in charge of trade. Beneath them are herders and artisans and at the bottom are labourers, who perform menial tasks. The labourers used to be unpaid slaves, but that custom has now been abolished.

Tagelmust

The climate of the Sahara is extreme. In summer, temperatures can climb to 50°C. In winter, they can drop below zero at night.

Tuareg men wear a distinctive blue veil to protect their eyes from the sand and sun and to prevent bad spirits from entering the body. This headscarf is called a *tagelmust*. It is made of an indigo cloth from Niger sewn together in strips.

Men begin wearing the veil at the age of 25, when they are ready to marry. The first veiling is performed in a special ritual by spiritual leader called a *marabout*.

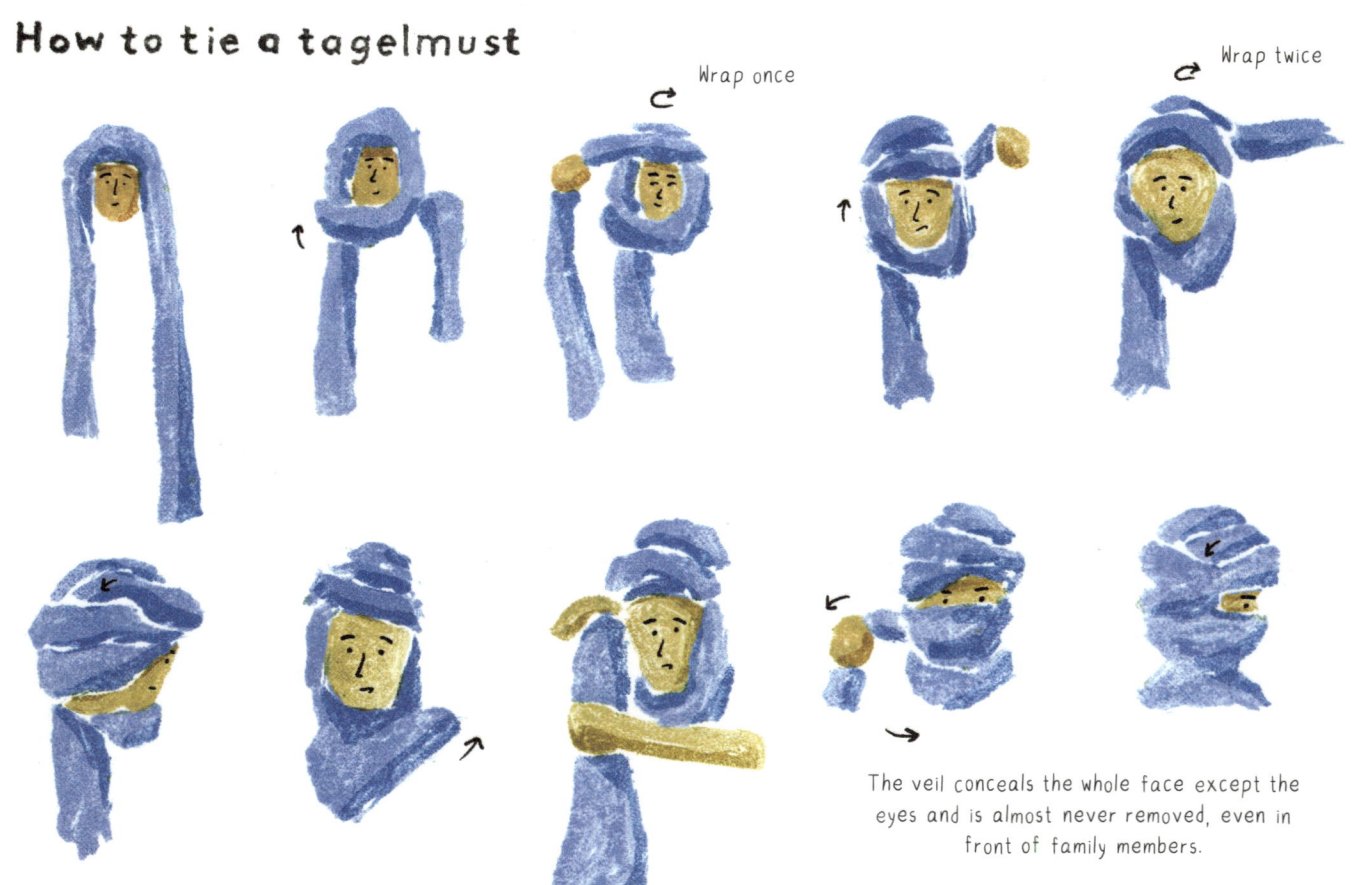

How to tie a tagelmust

Wrap once

Wrap twice

The veil conceals the whole face except the eyes and is almost never removed, even in front of family members.

Craft

The artisan class of the Tuareg, known as *inedan*, are known for their craftsmanship. Historically, they made almost everything that was necessary for daily life in the desert; tents, bags, saddles, swords, beds, musical instruments and jewellery. Their ornate silversmithing is much admired, and fetches a high price. In the past, a single pendant was worth a young camel.

The *tanaghilt* or Tuareg cross is a pendant necklace passed from father to son with the words "I will give you the four corners of the world because one cannot know where one will die."

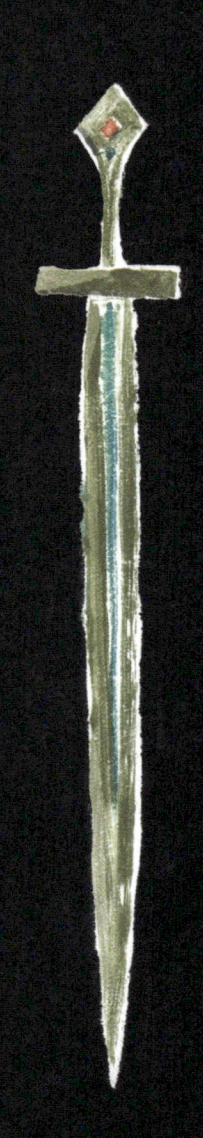

The *takoba* is a long sword with a double-edged blade. The Tuareg do not like touching iron, so the takoba's hilt is always fully covered.

Today

Climate change has caused the expansion of the Sahara, pushing the Tuareg into more populated areas to the north and south of the desert. Many have settled into towns, leaving their nomadic traditions behind. Others take on odd jobs as herdsmen or labourers to make a living.

In some countries, discrimination against the Tuareg is a problem, and Tuareg lands have been reclaimed by new governments.

In Niger, for example, Tuareg lands have been found to be rich in uranium. A lot of their territory has now been leased to mining companies that poison the lands with radioactive waste.

Some aspects of nomadic culture have managed to survive. The salt caravan routes run across Mali and Niger. Although much of the salt is now transported by truck, the long relationships between the Tuareg and the salt miners mean that the camel caravans still operate. The camels are loaded up with vast salt slabs weighing up to 150 kg before they set off on their 600 km journey.

Nenets

The Nenets are pastoral nomads that live in a remote corner of Siberia called the Yamal Peninsula, right near the Arctic Circle.

Every year, the Nenets move giant herds of reindeer across around 1,000 km of land, following the lichen and moss pastures on which the herds feed. In the summer, they follow the coastline of the Arctic Sea and in winter, when temperatures can reach -50°C, they travel south towards the forest. Part of the migration includes a 48 km crossing over the frozen waters of the Ob River.

The Yamal Peninsula is around 1.5 times the size of France

Ob River

'Yamal' in the language of the Nenets means 'the end of the world'.

Tundra is a vast, flat, treeless Arctic landscape. The subsoil is permanently frozen so only grasses and small shrubs can survive.

At certain times of the year, the Nenets will move camp every two days.

The trains of reindeer can stretch out for eight kilometres.

The Nenets were historically known as 'Samoyed'. This was a group term used by Russians to describe the all ethnic tribes that live in Northern Siberia. It translates literally as 'self eaters', and is now considered a derogatory name.

Living and believing

There are two groups of Nenets. The biggest group is the Tundra Nenets, who live far to the north. The Forest Nenets, or *Khandeyar*, are a smaller group living in the wooded region further south. They each speak a distinct language that the other group cannot understand.

However, they share a love for their reindeer, which are at the very heart of all Nenet life. They follow the natural migration patterns of reindeer, they eat reindeer meat, they wear reindeer fur and live in tents made of reindeer hide. Their tools and weapons are made using reindeer bone.

Nenet coats are called *malitsa* and they are worn with the fur on the inside. They are sewn together with reindeer sinew.

Reindeer meat is usually eaten raw, or sometimes cooked in a meat soup.

In the winter, men wear another layer of reindeer hide on top of their malitsa called a *gus*. This is so warm that they able to sleep outside in -50°C temperatures.

Reindeer are also an important part of the Nenet religion. It is believed that humans and reindeer have a sacred bond. The humans must protect the reindeer and accompany them on their migrations, whilst the reindeer offer themselves for food and transport. Every Nenet has their own personal sacred reindeer, which may not be harnessed or slaughtered until it is no longer able to walk.

Nenets believe in many gods, who look after the land and its resources. During their travels, the Nenets carry carved wooden dolls, bear skins and lucky coins on a holy sledge. The contents of this special sledge are only unpacked by the tribe elders on special occasions or for religious rituals.

Nenets pass their traditions on in stories and songs sung by a shaman called a *tadibya*. Sometimes drums are used to help the shamans enter a trance-like state.

Tent life

Nenet tents care called *chums*. They have a similar design to a Native American tipi. Long wooden poles are organised in a cone-shape and reindeer skins are wrapped around them. Each family lives in their own chum, sleeping close together on the ground.

The frame is made of 33 fir poles measuring around four metres each.

Once the structure is built, the heavy skins are positioned with the help of pulleys and ropes.

A stove is used for heating and cooking. The smoke escapes through a hole in the roof.

In the winter, the tent has floorboards, but in the summer these are taken away and left on sledges in the tundra, to be collected on the return journey.

Sledges carrying food and possessions are arranged in half circles around the chums. The sacred sledge with its wooden doll-gods is positioned behind the chum of the tribe leader, pointing directly at its centre.

Nenets often take a stick with them to the toilet to fend off any overly friendly reindeer!

In the winter, the Nenets fish through ice holes using large nets that are set beneath the ice. Nenet fishermen can sometimes be seen plunging their hands in ice cold water to warm them up!

33

Future

Under the pastures of the Arctic tundra lie huge deposits of oil and natural gas – almost a quarter of the world's reserves. In recent years, thousands of exploration drill sites have popped up on Nenet land and a new railroad now connects the remote Yamal Peninsula to other parts of Russia.

This has been a mixed blessing for the Nenets. The mining has caused environmental damage to the quality of the grazing lands, and mining infrastructure has blocked some migration routes. However, it has also brought financial stability to the population. As the opportunities increase, young Nenets are choosing to stay on the tundra, rather than leaving nomadic life behind.

Climate change has had an impact on the Nenets. Warmer summers affect plant growth and later winters delay the times at which the nomads and their herds can cross the frozen rivers. However, Nenets maintain a flexible outlook and adjust to the new realities as best they can, organising activism groups to protect their rights from the threats they face.

Roma

The Roma, or Romani, people are a large community of nomads that can be found across Europe and the Americas.

It is thought that the original Romani population came from Rajasthan, India, and then migrated through Persia (today's Iran), reaching the Balkans in Eastern Europe in around the 10th century. There is very little written history of the Roma people, so the exact timeline is unclear, however, the Romani language has close roots to the Indian language of Sanskrit.

There are about 12 million people worldwide who identify as Roma, with about seven million of those in Europe. The largest Roma populations live in Romania and Bulgaria.

Tattare (Norway)

Romanichal (UK)

Manouche (France)

Cale (Spain)

Throughout history, there has been frequent tension between the Romani people and the settled populations of the countries that they travel through. Romani people call non-Roma people *gadje* which translates as 'bumpkin' or 'barbarian'. They in turn are often called names like 'gypsy' or 'tsigane', which are considered offensive.

Travelling

The Romani people usually travel along routes that have been established for hundreds of years. Traditional stopping places are called 'atching tans' and are often on land where medieval landowners once provided food and shelter in return for manual labour. New landowners may not be so generous, and this can be a cause of friction.

Sinti (Germany)

The word 'Roma' has nothing to do with Romania or roaming. Rom simply means 'man' in Romani. The Romani are known by different names in different countries.

Sansis (Kazakhstan)

Kowli (Iran)

Sikligars (Northern India)

In the winter, the Roma stop travelling and stay in one place, which they return to every year. This is the place that a family is 'from'.

Ghagar (Egypt)

Luri (Middle East)

Banjara (Southern India)

37

Living

Originally, the Romani would travel in horse-drawn carts, pitching tents made of bent hazel branches called 'benders'. In the mid-19th century, they started using brightly coloured four-wheel wagons called *vardos*.

A vardo is decorated with elaborate carvings and brightly painted pictures of Roma life. Inside, it has built-in seats, a wardrobe and bunks at the back. Most have a small cast-iron cooking stove with a chimney. They don't have a toilet, as it against Roma tradition to have a toilet inside living quarters.

The vardos were pulled using a special breed of horse called a 'gypsy cob'.

Although Roma people now mostly live and travel in caravans or trailers, the beautiful craftsmanship of the vardos makes them highly prized, and the 'Age of the Vardos', which lasted from 1840 to around 1920, is thought of as a high point in Roma history.

Religion and traditions

Romani people tend to take on the religious beliefs of the countries they live in. Romani people in Croatia and Bulgaria will be Christian, whilst Romani bands in Serbia and Albania will be Muslim. More important than the religion itself is the *Romanipen*, a Romani world view in which nomadic traditions and family are of the utmost importance.

Family

Patriarchal family values are at the heart of Romani life. Men are expected to work and earn money, whilst women look after children and home. When a couple marries, the man's family pays a 'bride price' to the woman's family, and then takes her in for a few years so that she may learn their ways before the couple moves out on their own.

The bonds between family units are very strong. An extended family is called a *vitsa*, and a group of vitsas that travel together is called a band. Loyalty and mutual respect are very important within the band. If a dispute erupts between band members, they will present their cases in front of the *kris*, which is the traditional court of the Roma people. If a person is found guilty, they might be made to do menial tasks, or in serious cases, they might be expelled from the band.

Work

The Romani people have traditionally worked in jobs that suit their mobile lifestyles; livestock traders, musicians, circus entertainers, tinkers and metalsmiths. Today, rather than selling livestock, they sometimes sell used cars, and rather than working as metalsmiths they often work as car mechanics and labourers.

Music and entertainment are an important part of Romani work and life. Many folk traditions across central Europe have been kept alive in Romani dances and songs. The *lautari*, for example, are Romani musicians who play at weddings across Romania and Bulgaria. Their improvised, complex harmonies have influenced the music of many classical and jazz musicians throughout Europe over the years.

Many famous folk dances, such as the flamenco of Spain, are said to have originated in Romani culture.

Future

The Roma people face many challenges. Although many have now settled down, they remain the most disadvantaged ethnic minority in Europe, with the highest rates of illiteracy, unemployment and malnutrition and the lowest life expectancy. Stigmas around the Romani lifestyle have led to open discrimination by settled peoples and their governments (prejudice against Romani people is called 'antiziganism'). The violent persecution of Romani people is not uncommon in parts of Eastern Europe. In some countries, Roma children must attend special schools, which often have very low standards.

Roma people are now rising up to fight the injustices. Growing numbers of young activists and university educated leaders are helping to organise communities and demand political action and social change.

Maasai

The Maasai people are pastoral nomads, following their great cattle herds across the open savannah of Eastern Africa's Great Rift Valley.

Originally hailing from South Sudan, the Maasai migrated into Kenya and Northern Tanzania in the 15th century. They were powerful warriors, and by the 1800s, they ruled a large territory. However, drought, disease and colonialism halved their land and population by the early 20th century.

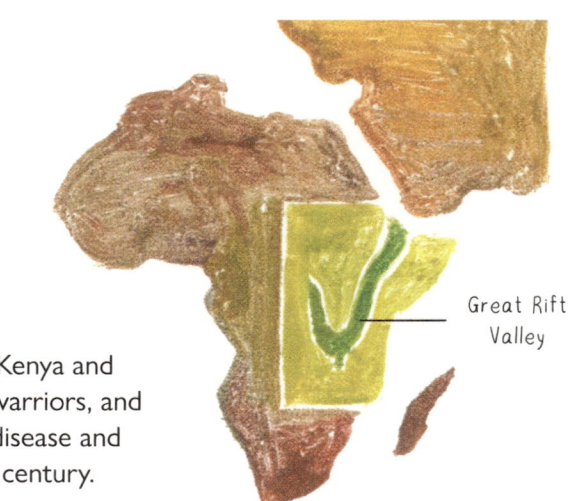

Great Rift Valley

Savannah is a vast, grassy plain with scattered trees. Young male warriors are responsible for herding the cattle across the grasslands with the changing seasons, giving the land time to regenerate.

Today, the Maasai number about one million. Although this only accounts for two percent of the Kenyan population, they are internationally renowned for their proud heritage and distinctive traditions, which they have fought to preserve over the centuries. They speak a language called Maa, which has its roots in the Nile Valley.

The Maasai are experts with spears and clubs. The Maasai club is called an *orinka*. It can be accurately thrown from a distance of 100 m.

Living

The Maasai house, called an *inkajijik*, is an oval-shaped framework of woven poles and branches, plastered with mud, grass, cow dung, urine and ash. The family cooks, eats and sleeps inside the small space, which measures only around five square metres.

The houses are built around an enclosure in which all the livestock are kept at night. A thorny fence keeps wild animals out.

Cattle is at the heart of Maasai life. Families and clans create alliances through the exchange of cattle; a man's wealth is measured by the size of his herd and a Maasai diet relies on the milk, uncooked meat and, occasionally, blood of their cattle. As herds have grown smaller, crops such as rice, potatoes and cabbage have become more important.

Clothing and accessories

The most famous Maasai garment is the *shuka*. This is a thick, woven cotton blanket worn around the shoulders. It was adopted in the 1960s to replace animal skins. The shukas are often red, a colour that symbolises bravery and the blood of cattle. Maasai men near the coast wear a stripy sarong called a *kikoi*. The women wear a wrap called a *kanga*.

It is common for Maasai men and women to pierce and stretch their earlobes, in which they wear long metal and beaded hoops.

The Maasai are known for their elaborate beadwork, and they often wear many layers of brightly coloured beaded necklaces, neck discs and bracelets. The complex patterns of the beadwork can convey information about the age or position of the wearer within the tribe.

Only senior warriors are allowed to wear their hair long and they often braid their hair in complex styles, sometimes using ochre to dye their hair and skin red. Warriors have also been known to scar their bodies with heated spears to show bravery.

Dancing

The Maasai are known for their jumping dance, called the *adamu*, which is usually held at the end of a special ceremony called *eunoto*; the graduation of a boy to a warrior. In this ritual, *morani* (junior warriors) stand in a semicircle, chanting rhythmically.

Each young man takes a turn to jump several times straight up in the air, often reaching over half a metre in height. The rest of the warriors sway to the music, moving their heads back and forth.

Maasai society is organised in a hierarchy of age. At 14, young men are known as *morani*, or junior warriors. They live in isolation in the bush, learning tribal customs and endurance, as well as forming a connection to the land. Around the age of 30 they will become senior warriors. At 45 they become junior elders, and at around 60 they become senior elders, who can make decisions for the tribe.

Religion and traditions

The Maasai god is called Engai. When Engai is in a benevolent mood, he is called Engai Narok (Black God). When he is angry and vengeful, he is called Engai Na-nyokie (Red God).

The Maasai believe that Engai created all cattle for them to look after. Some Maasai have taken on Christian or Islamic beliefs alongside their belief in Engai.

The totem of the Maasai people is the lion. In the past, young men would have to kill a lion as part of their initiation ceremony into adulthood.

Today, lion hunting has been banned, but occasionally the Maasai will still kill a lion who has harmed their herd. A man who kills a lion is considered a great hero.

Future

Like all nomadic cultures, the Maasai are having to adjust to modern problems. Much of the Maasai land has been taken over by private farms, wildlife parks and government projects. The land that they retain is the driest and least fertile, and it is most vulnerable to climate change. Drought is a regular occurrence, and herds have shrunk to a fraction of their previous size.

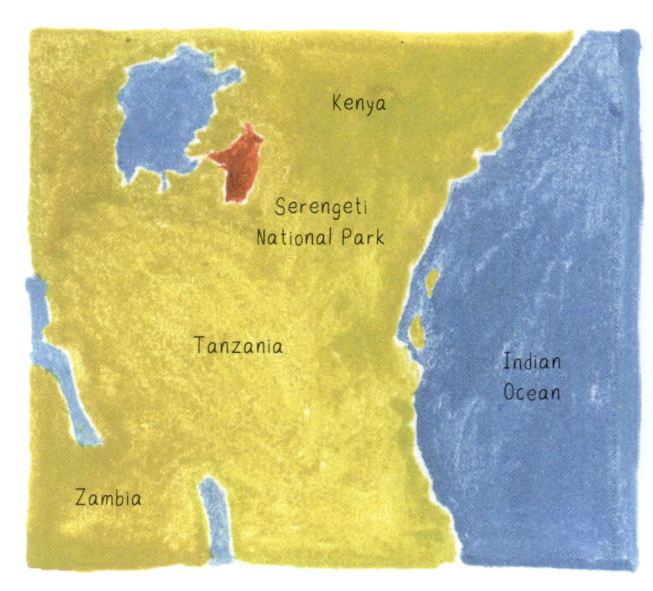

Maasai land once covered over 300,000 km². It is now a fraction of that size.

The governments of Kenya and Tanzania actively encouraged the Maasai to settle down, and many Maasai left their nomadic lifestyles behind.

Tourism has provided a new source of income. The Maasai sell their jewellery and share their deep knowledge of the land with travellers. This can come at a price, as ancient traditions can be devalued when they are simplified and made accessible to outsiders.

However, the Maasai have shown great resilience, holding onto their unique identity, and selecting which elements of modernity to accept or reject. In the past 25 years, the Maasai population has doubled in size, and communities have become more organised at speaking out and protecting Maasai rights.

Sama-Bajau

The Sama-Bajau are sea-faring nomads living off the coasts of the Philippines, Malaysia and Indonesia. They make a living from spear fishing and from selling marine products like seaweed and shells.

Philippines

Malaysia

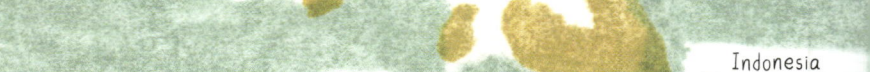

Indonesia

For over 1,000 years, the Sama-Bajau lived in wooden houseboats called *lepa*, coming ashore only to sell their wares or to shelter from storms.

There are many sub-groups of Sama-Bajau, each with their own customs and variation of the Sinama language. The groups can be divided into two main categories:

The land-based Sama (Sama-Dilaya), who live in houses and the sea-based Sama (Sama-Dilaut), who traditionally live on the sea, coming ashore only occasionally.

Living

A *lepa* is a traditional Sama houseboat, which was once the only home the sea nomads would know.

A cooking hearth is located at the back of the boat.

A single sail is mounted on a mast at the front of the boat

There are often lots of beautiful, flowery carvings on the lepa. These are called *okil*.

A detachable 'house' is built in the centre of the hull with a roof made of plaited palm leaves.

The hull of the lepa is made of a dugout (a hollowed out tree), with wood planks curving upwards.

In the past, when a young man was to be married, his family would build him a lepa. Upon his death, the lepa would be taken apart and the dugout would be used as his coffin.

Today, most Sama-Bajau live in wooden houses raised up on stilts over the shallow coastal waters. The houses are connected to one another by narrow wooden bridges. They are often densely crowded. Lepas are still used, but not as primary accommodation.

Inside, the house usually has one big room and a kitchen attached.

Fishing

The Sama-Bajau hunt for fish using spears or spear guns. In a normal day, a Bajau person might spend more than five hours under water.

With no equipment but a pair of hand carved wooden goggles, the Sama-Bajau can free-dive to depths of 70 metres, staying under water for up to 13 minutes at a time!

Scientists discovered that the Sama-Bajau have evolved to have larger spleens, which maximises the flow of oxygen through the body, allowing them to stay under water for longer than seems humanly possible.

Some Sama-Bajau deliberately puncture their eardrums to reduce the build-up of pressure in their ears under water.

Religion

Although most Sama-Bajau now practice Islam, they also hold onto some earlier religious beliefs.

Sama ancestors are called *umboh*. The umboh are responsible for the luck of the sea, granting good favours or causing accidents. Each boat has its own guardian spirit, who must be appeased if its owner wants good fortune.

The Sama-Bajau tell an origin story in which they once lived on land. The king of the land had a daughter, who was swept out to sea in a terrible storm. The Sama-Bajau were ordered to find her, but no matter how hard they looked, they couldn't track her down.

Rather than return and face the wrath of the king, the Sama-Bajau stayed at sea, nomadic forever more.

Future

The nomadic lifestyle of the Sama-Bajau people is gradually disappearing. Commercial fishing trawlers have made it impossible to make a living from spear fishing, and some Bajau have resorted to destructive methods to make ends meet, including blast fishing, cyanide fishing and coral mining.

Lepas are harder to maintain and construct. They were once made of trees with light wood, but as those trees are now endangered, heavier wood must be used, which means that the lepas have to be equipped with motors, making them more expensive and less environmentally-friendly.

As more of the nomads come ashore, communities of stilt houses grow ever bigger, resulting in poor living conditions and friction with local populations.

Yanomami

The Yanomami are one of the last remaining American Indian (Amerindian) tribes of the Amazon rainforest. They live in small villages in the border area between Brazil and Venezuela.

The Yanomami are semi-nomadic. The soil of the Amazon is not very fertile, so every four to five years, when their crops begin to die, the Yanomami community will move their village to another location.

There are about 38,000 Yanomami people known of today. They do not identify themselves as a single nation, but as a collection of individual communities.

Traditional Yanomami culture encourages aggressive behaviour, and they are fearsome warriors. Much of Yanomami life centres on trading with communities that are considered friendly and waging violent war against groups who are not.

Everybody in the community is considered equal. Each Yanomami community has a 'leader' called a *tuxawa*, but important decisions are made democratically.

Living

A Yanomami community will live in one big woven structure called a *shanobo*, which takes the shape of an oval with an open centre. The shanobo is made up of individual units which each house one family. These units sometimes have their own roofs, but never have solid walls between them.

At night, the Yanomami sleep in hammocks near the fire.

The central area is used for rituals, feasts and games.

Surrounding the shanobo are garden plots, where the Yanomami grow cassava and plantains. They rely on these plots for most of their food, which is why they need to move when they are no longer fertile.

Clothing

The Yanomami have distinctive facial piercings. Thin rods of bone or wood go through their ears, noses, lips and cheeks, and are sometimes decorated with feathers.

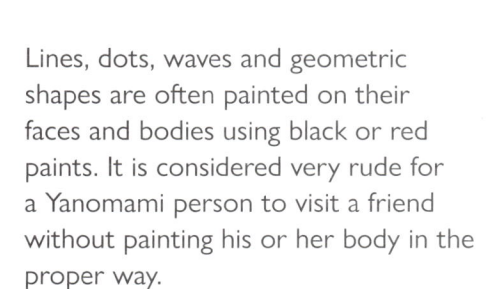

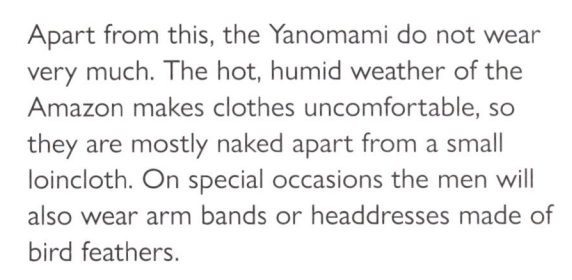

Lines, dots, waves and geometric shapes are often painted on their faces and bodies using black or red paints. It is considered very rude for a Yanomami person to visit a friend without painting his or her body in the proper way.

Apart from this, the Yanomami do not wear very much. The hot, humid weather of the Amazon makes clothes uncomfortable, so they are mostly naked apart from a small loincloth. On special occasions the men will also wear arm bands or headdresses made of bird feathers.

Food

The crops that the Yanomami grow make up most of their diet, but they also hunt, fish and gather herbs and edible insects from the rainforest. They are known for their incredible knowledge of rainforest plants. Over 500 plants are regularly used for food and medicine.

The Yanomami fish using a special poison made of pounded vines. The poison stuns the fish, which rise to the surface and are scooped up in baskets.

Only a small portion of the food that the Yanomami eat is meat. A hunter won't eat an animal that he has killed. He gives it to the rest of the tribe and is given meat by another hunter.

Yanomami women weave baskets, which they use for foraging. The baskets are dyed red with the juice of a berry called *onoto*.

Religion

The spiritual world is very important to the Yanomami. Every creature, rock, tree and mountain has a spirit called a *xapripe*.

The shaman of the community will eat a poisonous plant that makes him have visions and allows him to communicate with the xapripes.

Future

The Yanomami are at great threat from the modern world. In the 1970s, a road was built through the northern frontier of the Amazon allowing loggers and ranchers to access areas that had previously been out of bounds. Big parts of the rainforest were then cleared for grazing lands.

Gold-miners called *garimpeiros* also came to the rainforest to seek their fortunes. They brought with them violence and disease. The Yanomami have had little exposure to outside culture, so are very vulnerable to illness. With no access to health clinics, many communities were devastated by disease.

The Yanomami are now working with various organisations to raise awareness of their situation. They are fighting to have their land protected and to gain better access to healthcare.

Some Yanomami have left the rainforest and settled down, but other communities continue their traditional lifestyles. It is said that there are some Yanomami communities so deep in the rainforest that they have still never had contact with the outside world.

Moving... and changing

Nomadic cultures are on the front-line of some of the world's most pressing problems. Most nomads live in arid and semi-arid regions like deserts, steppe and tundra. These types of environments are not owned or farmed, and they cover big expanses; perfect for supporting a small, mobile population. These environments are also most at risk of the effects of climate change, and nomadic peoples like the Mongols or the Nenets are finding that terrible droughts or storms are making their ways of living much more difficult, whilst traditional travel routes are no longer offering their herds the same quality of vegetation that they once did.

There is another downside to these arid environments – they often harbour secret treasures in the form of natural gas, oil and precious minerals. The nomads are often moved away from their traditional grazing lands so that governments and private companies can access this hidden wealth. Sometimes, the surrounding lands are poisoned with the waste from the mining activities.

Nomadic ways of life do not fit easily into traditionally organised society, and they are often viewed with suspicion by settled people, who look down on them as 'uncivilised' and see them as a threat to their safety. In certain instances, governments force nomads to settle down, or encourage open discrimination.

Despite this bleak outlook, there is still hope for nomadic peoples. As travellers, they have, throughout history, absorbed other cultures as they moved around, and there is often an openness and flexibility to nomadic peoples, which allows them to adapt to new situations and circumstances. Many nomadic cultures have embraced aspects of modern life, such as cars, trucks, internet and solar technologies to make their lives and livelihoods easier to manage. In some instances, when governments have been more respectful of nomadic rights, they have benefited from the riches beneath their lands.

In today's world, there are lots of people who have an unusual relationship with the idea of 'home'. Political migrants and refugees have been forced into situations where they have no permanent homes. There are also many people today who live a less settled life out of choice. A rising cost of living, and a questioning of capitalist values has led some to choose more mobile lives in camper-vans or similar. Some people call themselves 'digital nomads' – they work remotely while travelling to new places and experiencing new cultures.

This does not make them nomads, who follow ancient routes year on year, and who have built a way of living around travelling. However, it does raise awareness of the difficulties that face communities who live outside traditional social structures. It has also helped people appreciate alternative lifestyles that are less materialistic and more in touch with nature and landscape.

A growing interest in nomadic culture has led to an increase in tourism. Nomadic societies that were once isolated from the outside world are no longer so. Although tourism can be valuable, helping the nomads support themselves and educating outsiders about ancient customs, it can also be harmful. Nomadic communities that come to rely on tourism rely less on their traditional ways of living. Simplifying and glamorising meaningful aspects of life can devalue them.

The communities that we have learned about are marginalised – that means that they are on the margins of society and are therefore very vulnerable. It's important that we protect these cultures, because if we lose them, we also lose a vital connection to the roots of human history and to an alternative, more sustainable way of being.

Which of these dwellings would you most like to live in?

These are some of the essential items that nomads travel with.
What are the belongings you would take with you that you definitely can't live without?

Glossary

Adamu	A Maasai dance in which young warriors take turns jumping very high in the air.
Airag	A drink made from fermented mare's milk drunk by Mongolian nomads.
Amghar	A Tuareg chief.
Atai	Tuareg green tea.
Atching tan	A Romani stopping off place.
Buuz	Mongolian meat dumplings.
Chum	A cone-shaped Nenet tent that looks a bit similar to a tipi.
Del	A heavy, tunic-like coat worn by Mongolian nomads.
Dzud	A Mongolian weather pattern in which a hot, dry summer is followed by a harsh winter, causing devastation to herds of livestock.
Eunoto	A ceremony to celebrate the graduation of young Maasai warriors.
Ger	A circular yurt used by Mongolian nomads.
Gus	An overcoat worn by Nenets in winter.
Inedan	Tuareg craftsmen known for their skilled silversmithing.
Inkajijik	A loaf-shaped Maasai mud hut.
Khandeyar	Nenets living in Siberian forests south of the Yamal Peninsula.
Khorkhog	Mongolian meat casserole.
Kris	The traditional court of the Romani peoples.
Lautari	Romani folk musicians in Eastern Europe.
Lepa	A houseboat used by the Sama-Bajau that used to be their only home.
Malitsa	Reindeer-skin coats worn by Nenet nomads.
Moran	A junior Maasai warrior.
Okil	Elaborate carvings that decorate the lepa boats of the Sama-Bajau.
Orinka	A Maasai club that can be thrown from over 100 metres.
Romanipen	A Romani world view with nomadic traditions and family values at its heart.
Shagai	Sheep anklebones used like dice by Mongolian nomads.
Shanobo	A woven structure that is the communal living space for the Yanomami people.
Shuka	A thick, woven cotton blanket worn around the shoulders of the Maasai.
Steppe	Large areas of flat, unforested grassland, which covers much of Mongolia.
Tadibya	A Nenet shaman.
Tagelmust	An indigo headscarf worn by Tuareg men.
Takoba	A long, straight Tuareg sword.
Tanaghilt	A Tuareg cross necklace symbolising the four corners of the earth.
Toono	The opening in the roof of a Mongolian ger (yurt).
Tuxawa	A Yanomami leader.
Umboh	The holy ancestors of the Sama-Bajau.
Vardo	A highly decorated Romani wagon.
Vitsa	An extended Romani family.
Xapripe	Yanomami ancestors and spirits, who are said to communicate with the tribe's shaman.